To Larry:

Hold on to your dream. Someday our Church will be filled with Children like these.

You are so special to us and we know you will be home soon and we can have more good times together!

Our Love; L_____ _____.

Gary & Betty

Christmas 1995

The Children's
Christmas Pageant

The Cast

Mary	Krista Titus		Mandi Green
			Jesse Randall
Joseph	Ethan Green		Andrew Ackles
Baby Jesus	Nelson Kling	**Angels**	Danya Greene
			Scott Alvord
The Herald	Andrew Gilmore		Jamie Kerr
			Evan Alvord
Innkeepers	Tommy Giacomini		Sara Frank
	Travis Green		Katy Bridges
	Cara Giacomini		Jessica Titus
			Anne Linton
Shepherds	Lenwood Franklin		Willie Bridges
	Crystal Giacomini		Jenna Randall
	Aaron Bridges		

Set Design by Judy Howard

Library of Congress Cataloging-in-Publication Data

MacKenzie, Joy.
   The children's Christmas pageant.
   Summary: A retelling of the birth of Jesus through
text and photographs of children putting on a Christmas
pageant.
   1. Jesus Christ—Nativity—Juvenile literature.
[1. Jesus Christ—Nativity. 2. Bible stories—N.T.]
I. Frank, Marjorie. II. Briscoe, Christopher,
1951-   ill. III. Title.
BT315.2.M25 1989   232.92   89-11047
ISBN 0-8249-8395-5

Copyright © 1989 by Marjorie Frank and Joy MacKenzie
All rights reserved.
Published by Ideals Publishing Corporation
Nashville, Tennessee
Printed and bound in the United States of America.

ISBN 0-8249-8395-5

The Children's
Christmas Pageant

By Marjorie Frank and Joy MacKenzie
Photography By Christopher Briscoe

IDEALS CHILDREN'S BOOKS

Christmas began a long time ago. The story of how it happened is true and has not changed for hundreds of years—even though it has been told over and over again, by all kinds of people, in many languages.

Here it is told as it was recorded in the Holy Bible by a doctor named Luke. You have probably heard Dr. Luke's words before, but never quite like this because this time the story is told especially for you.

Let's see . . . We'll need
angels and shepherds
and sheep . . .

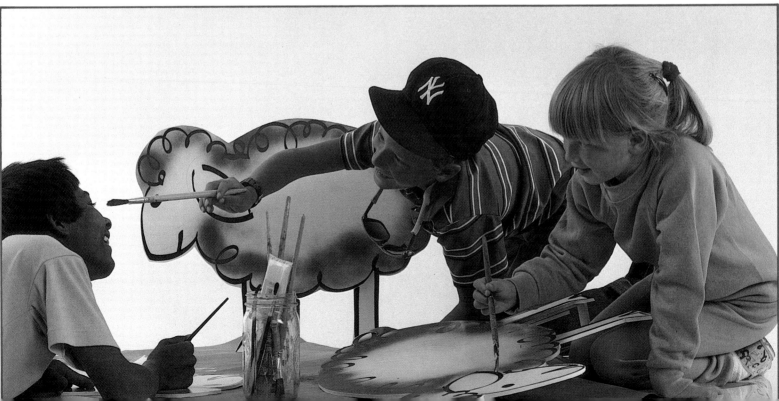

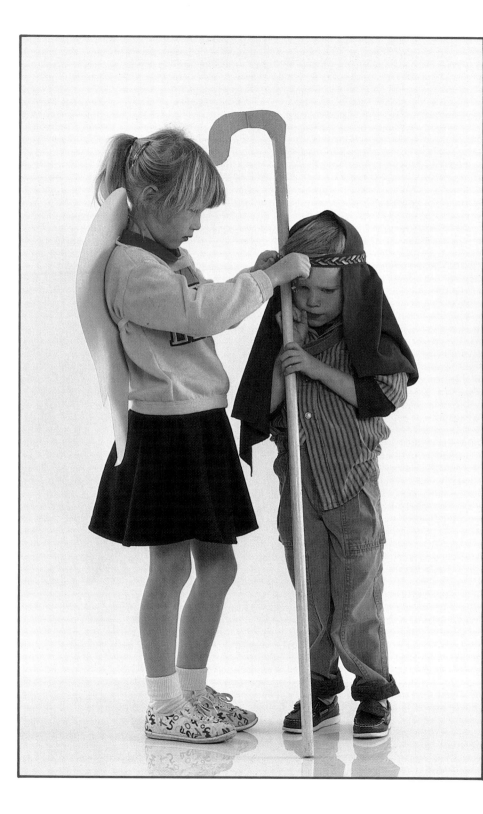

and a baby, of course!

We'll build a fine stable with cows and a donkey. And we'll tell the story better than ever before.

You'll see. It'll be great!

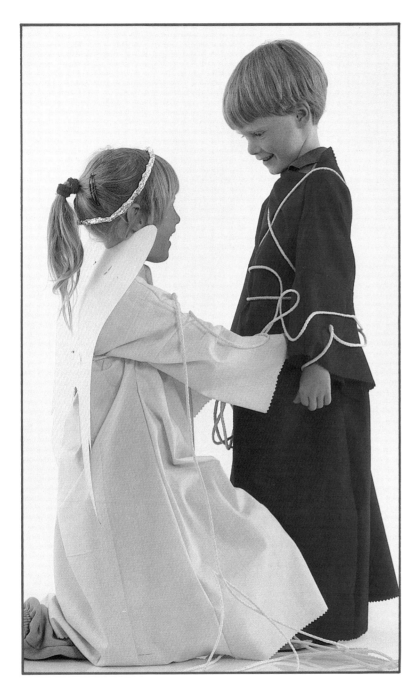

Do real heralds have this much trouble getting dressed?

See, angels *can* fly!

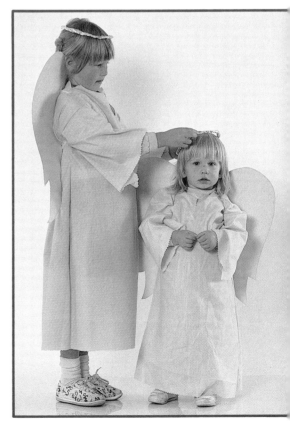

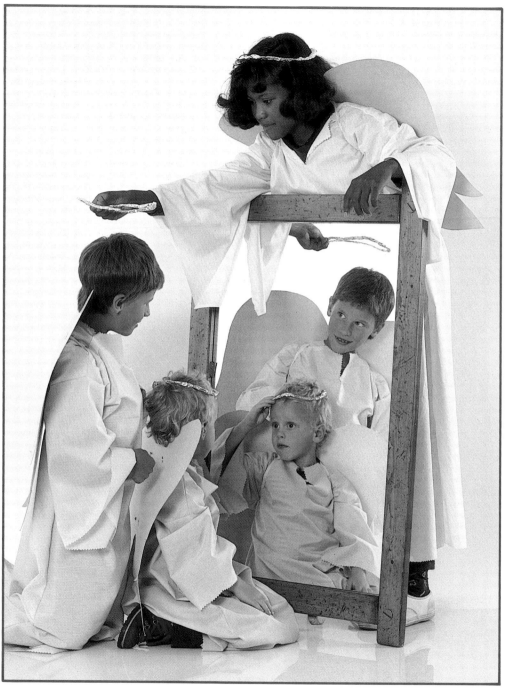

Is everybody ready?   It's showtime!

Tan Tan Ta Rah!

A golden trumpet sounds! "Listen everyone. Caesar has an announcement!"

Caesar wanted to know how many people lived in his empire. All families had to go to be counted in the place where their fathers were born. No exceptions!

Now, several months earlier, an angel had come to tell a young woman named Mary that she would be the mother of God's Son. Mary could hardly believe it!

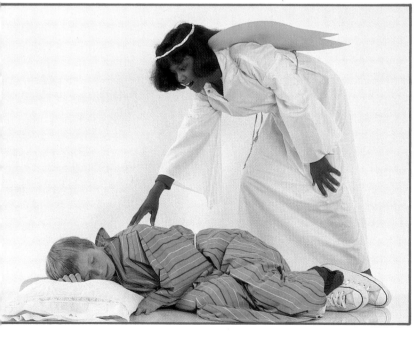

An angel had also visited Joseph, the man who would soon be Mary's husband. The angel told him that the baby should be named Jesus.

Joseph's father was from the city of Bethlehem, so Joseph and Mary had to make the long trip from their home in Nazareth to be counted in Bethlehem.

They were very tired when they reached Bethlehem, and Joseph began to look for a hotel room where they could rest.

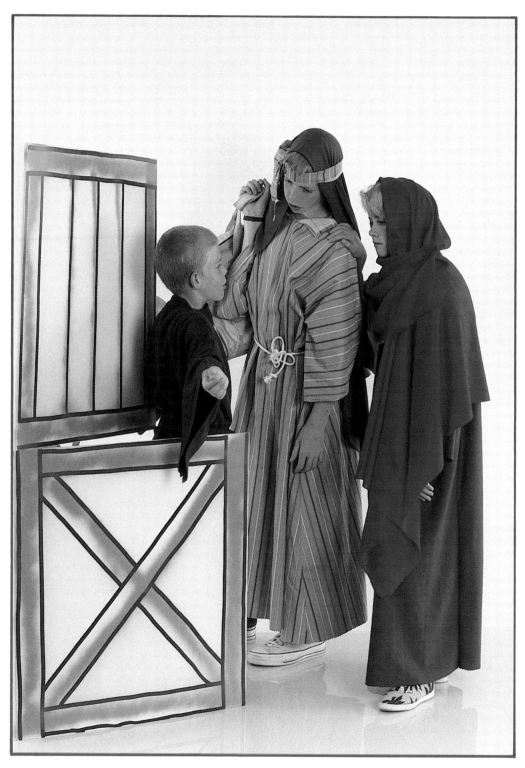

But the city was full of people who had come to be counted. There was no room.

Finally, a kind innkeeper offered them a quiet place in a warm, dry stable.

And
while
they
were
there,
the
baby
arrived!

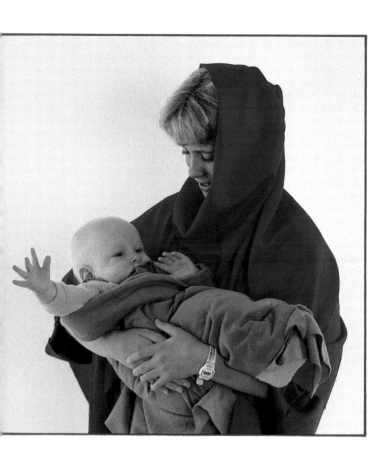

Mary and Joseph used clean cloths to wrap the baby, and they made him a bed in the animals' feedbox.

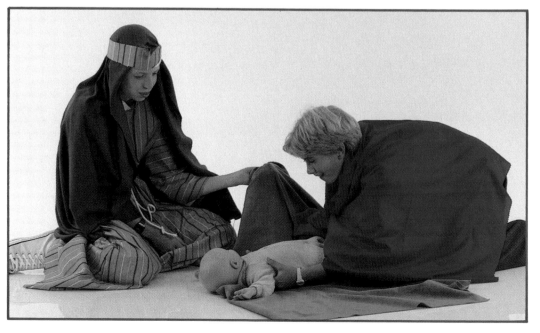

On that same night in the fields outside Bethlehem,

some sleepy shepherds were watching their sheep.

Suddenly, a bright light shone out of the darkness, and an angel appeared. The shepherds were scared to death!

But the angel said, "Don't be afraid. I have great news for you! A special baby is born in Bethlehem. He will grow up to be a king—the Savior of the world. You will find him wrapped in soft, clean cloths, lying in a manger."

Then . . .

Wow!

A whole bunch of angels appeared and started singing, "Glory to God in the highest!"

Leaping and dancing and praising God, they shouted,

"Peace on earth and joy to all people!"

Well, when the angels had finally disappeared into heaven, the excited shepherds looked at one another and said, "What are we waiting for? Let's get to Bethlehem—

—fast!"

The shepherds came to the stable where they found the baby, lying in a manger, just as the angels had said. Mary and Joseph stood nearby, watching over the newborn Jesus.

And when the shepherds had seen the baby, they hurried away, excitedly
telling everybody all that had happened.

But Mary kept all
these thoughts quietly
tucked away in her heart.

"Joy to the world!

The Lord is come!"

They loved our story.

Take a bow, everyone!